HARCOURT HORIZONS

About My World

SOL Practice for Students

Orlando   Austin   Chicago   New York   Toronto   London   San Diego

Visit *The Learning Site!*
www.harcourtschool.com

Copyright © by Harcourt, Inc.

All rights reserved. No part of this publication may be reproduced or transmitted in any form or by any means, electronic or mechanical, including photocopy, recording, or any information storage and retrieval system, without permission in writing from the publisher.

Permission is hereby granted to individual teachers using the corresponding student's textbook or kit as the major vehicle for regular classroom instruction to photocopy Copying Masters from this publication in classroom quantities for instructional use and not for resale. Requests for information on other matters regarding duplication of this work should be addressed to School Permissions and Copyrights, Harcourt, Inc., 6277 Sea Harbor Drive, Orlando, Florida 32887-6777. Fax: 407-345-2418.

HARCOURT and the Harcourt Logo are trademarks of Harcourt, Inc., registered in the United States of America and/or other jurisdictions.

Photo Credits

Page placement Key: (t)-top (c)-center (b)-bottom (l)-left (r)-right (fg)-foreground (bg)-background.

20 The Virginian Pilot/Mort Fryman; 26 Bettmann/CORBIS; 28 Christie's Images/CORBIS; 30 Bettmann/CORBIS; 32(t) Stock Montage/Getty Images; 32(b) L0C; 34 CORBIS.

Printed in the United States of America

ISBN 0-15-337961-8

16 17 18 19 20   082   10 09 08

Contents

Maps and Globes
SOL 1.4a	Parts of a Map	1
SOL 1.5	Make a Map	2
SOL 1.4c, 1.4d	The State of Virginia	4
SOL 1.4c, 1.4d	The Capital of the United States	6

Economics
SOL 1.7	Difference Between Goods and Services	8
SOL 1.8, 1.9	Spend or Save?	9
SOL 1.7	People Are Buyers and Sellers	10

Good Citizenship
SOL 1.10b	Why Do We Have Rules?	12
SOL 1.10a	Being a Good Sport	14
SOL 1.10a	Showing Respect	15
SOL 1.10c	Working Hard in School	16
SOL 1.10d	Taking Responsibility	17
SOL 1.10e	Honesty and Truthfulness	18
SOL 1.12	United as Americans	20

Past and Present
SOL 1.1	Using a Time Line for Past and Present	21

Holidays
SOL 1.3	Columbus Day	22
SOL 1.3	Presidents' Day	24
SOL 1.3	Independence Day (Fourth of July)	25

Biographies
SOL 1.3	Christopher Columbus	26
SOL 1.2	George Washington	28
SOL 1.2	Benjamin Franklin	30
SOL 1.2	Abraham Lincoln	32
SOL 1.2	George Washington Carver	34

Name _____ Date _____

Parts of a Map

A map is a drawing that shows a place from above. On a map, symbols stand for something else. The map legend lists the symbols used on the map. It explains what the symbols stand for.

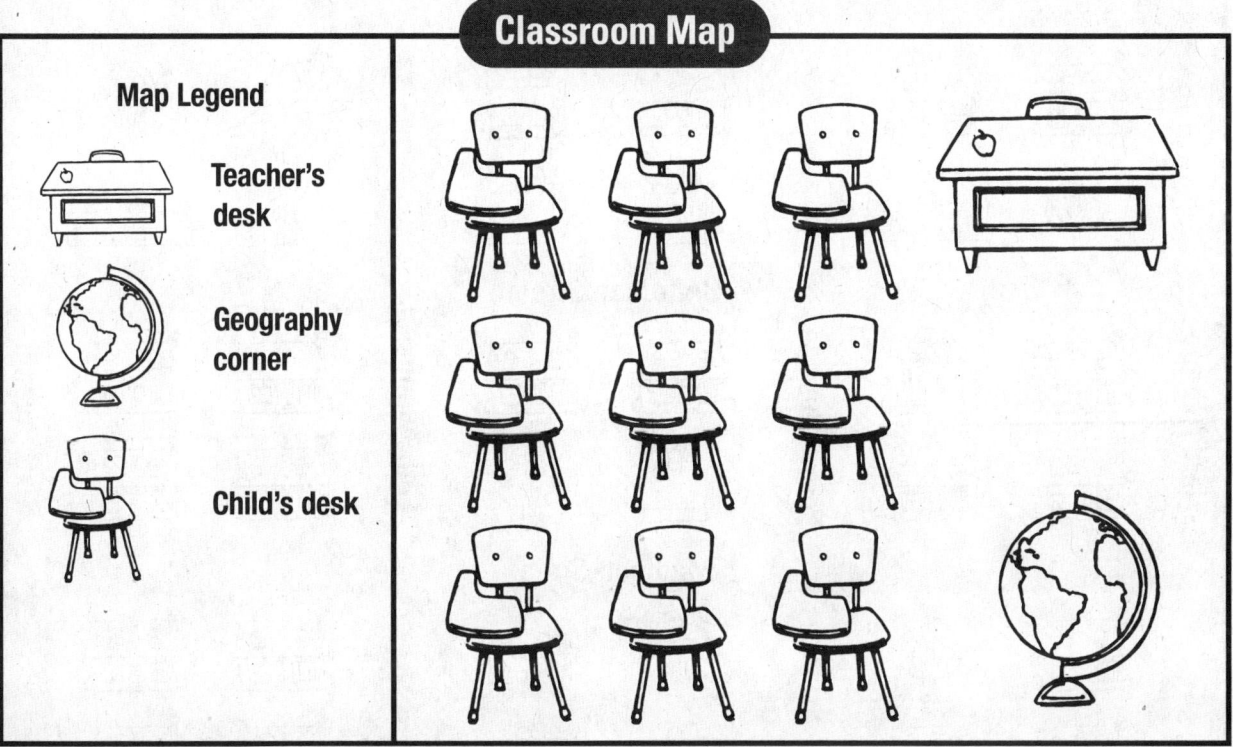

Review

1. What is the symbol for the Teacher's desk?

2. What does the 🌐 stand for on this map?

   Think of a symbol for a computer center. Draw the symbol in the map legend. Then add the symbol to the map.

SOL 1.4a
*Additional information has been provided to enhance the Standards of Learning.

Practice for Students ■ 1

Name _____ Date _____

Make a Map

This map shows a neighborhood. Look at the map legend. A map legend is a list of shapes and symbols used on a map and an explanation of what each stands for.

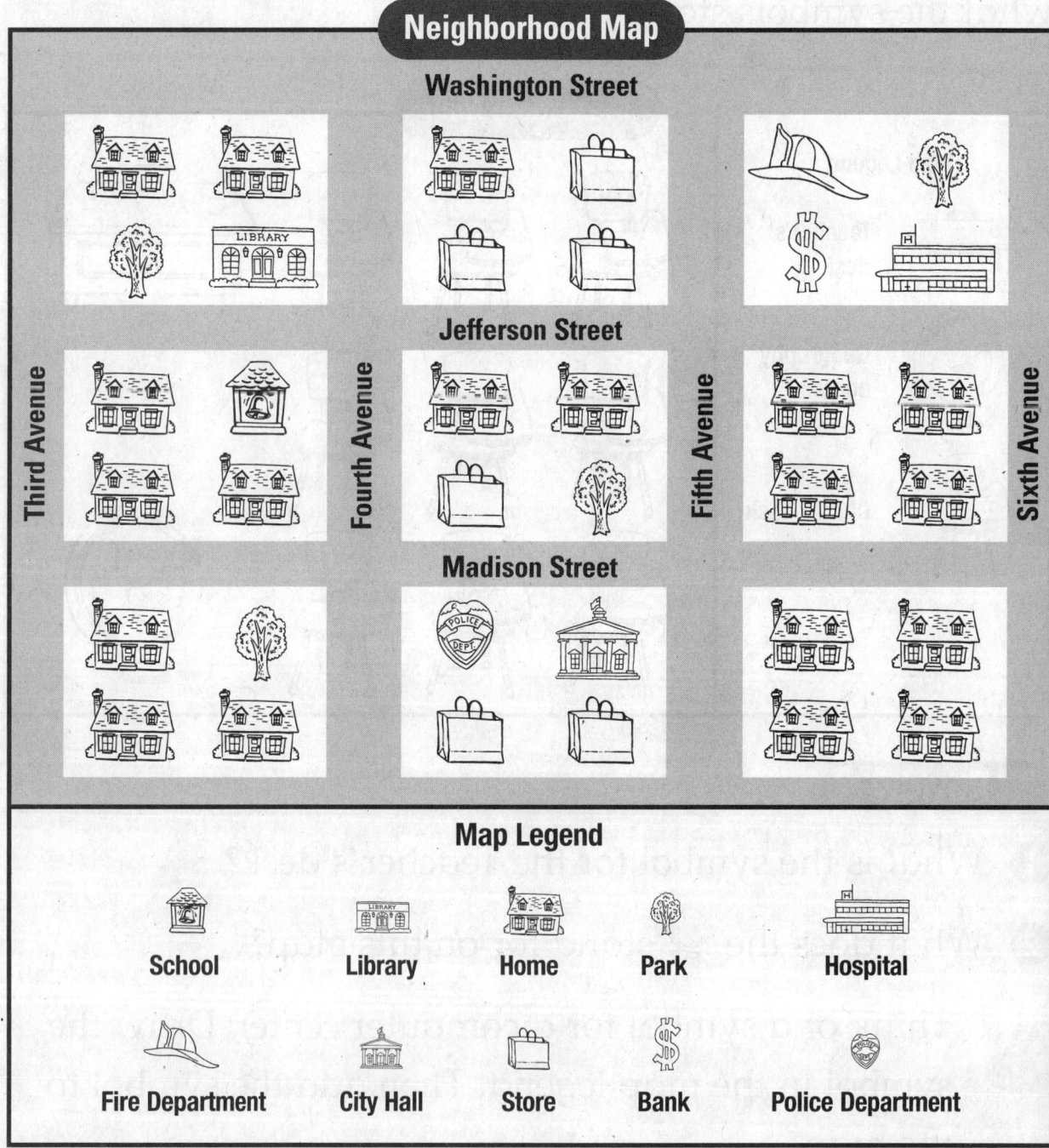

2 ■ Practice for Students

SOL 1.5
*Additional information has been provided to enhance the Standards of Learning.

Name _____ Date _____

Map Legend

Directions

Where are the stores in your neighborhood? What symbol would you use to stand for a store? Make a map of your neighborhood. Draw symbols to show where places are located. Make a legend to show what your symbols stand for.

SOL 1.5
*Additional information has been provided to enhance the Standards of Learning.

Name _____ Date _____

The State of Virginia

The United States of America is made up of 50 states. Each state has its own special shape.

This is the shape of the state of Virginia. Virginia is located on the east coast of our country. Can you find Virginia on this map?

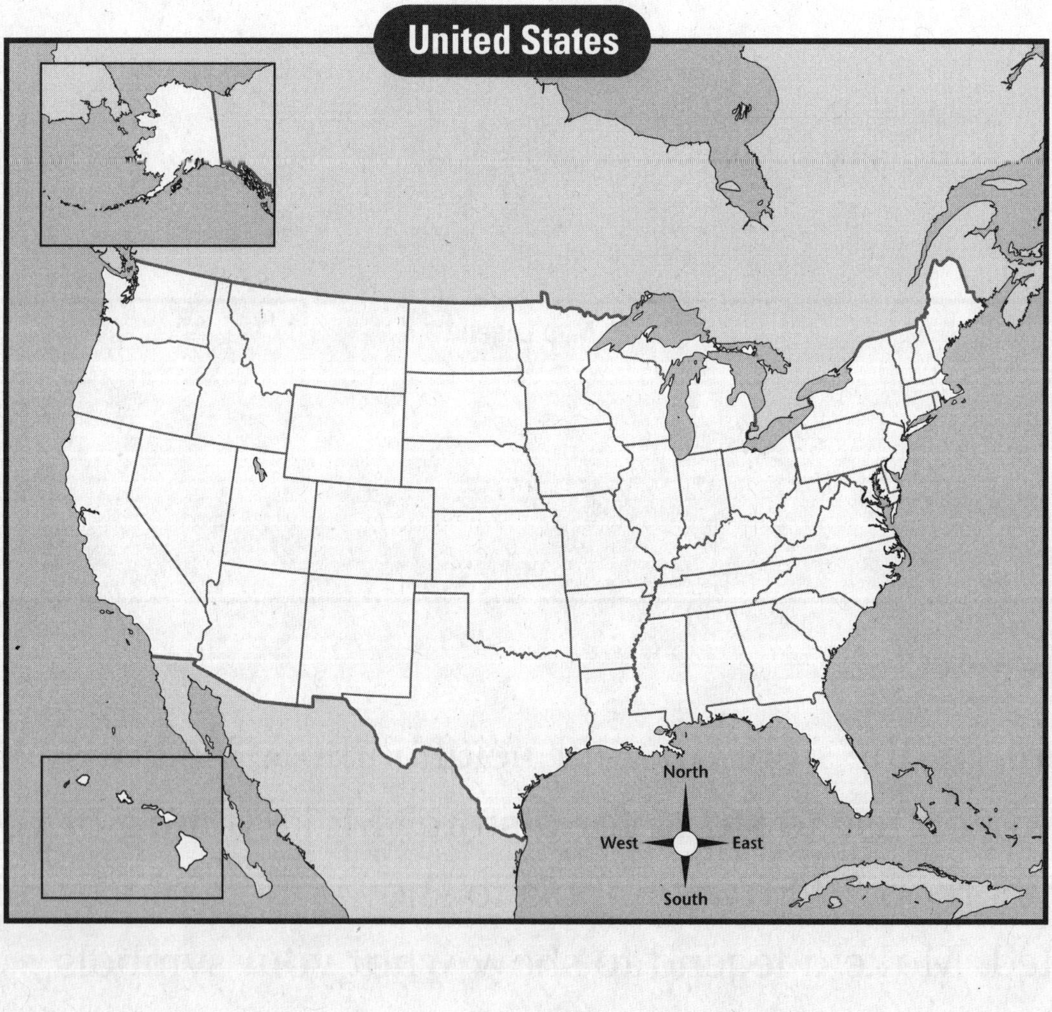

United States

4 ■ Practice for Students

SOL 1.4c, 1.4d
*Additional information has been provided to enhance the Standards of Learning.

Name _____ Date _____

You can tell by the shape that this is a map of Virginia. This map shows where some of the cities in Virginia are located. A ● shows where each city is. The capital city, Richmond, has a special symbol on the map. The ★ shows where Richmond is located.

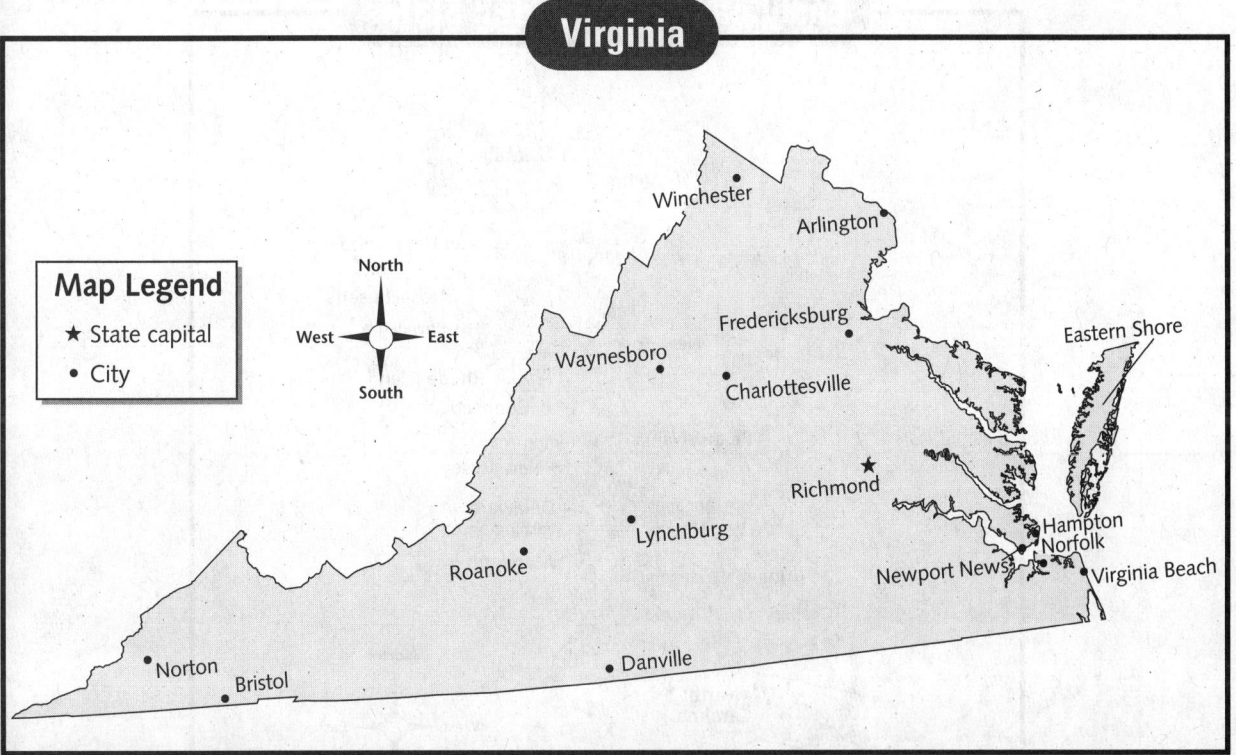

Directions

1. On the map on page 4, color the state of Virginia red.

2. Draw the shape of the state of Virginia. Draw a star where Richmond is located.

3. Draw an X where you live in Virginia.

SOL 1.4c, 1.4d
*Additional information has been provided to enhance the Standards of Learning.

Name _____ Date _____

The Capital of the United States

Each state has a capital city. The United States has a capital city, too. Our country's capital is Washington, D.C.

East Coast of the United States

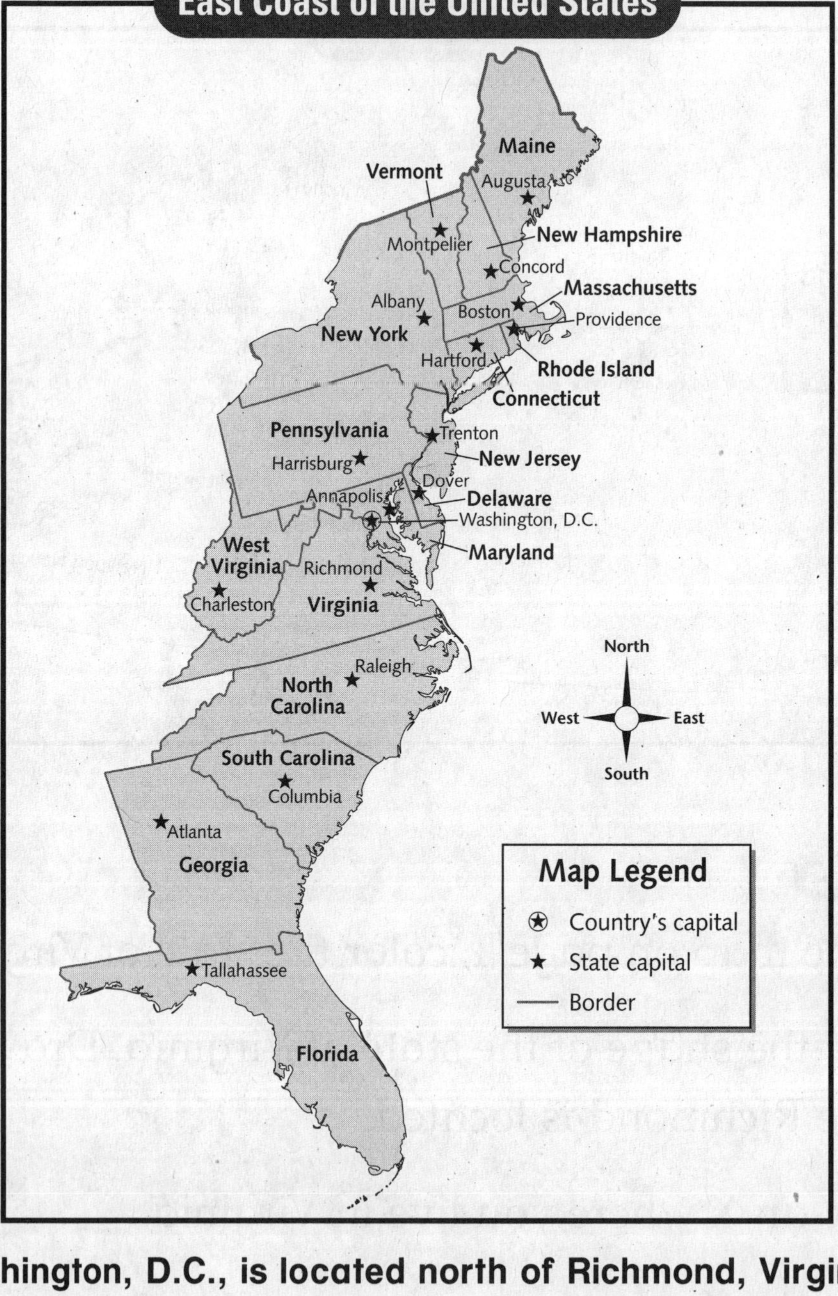

Map showing East Coast states with capitals marked: Augusta (Maine), Montpelier (Vermont), Concord (New Hampshire), Albany (New York), Boston (Massachusetts), Providence (Rhode Island), Hartford (Connecticut), Harrisburg (Pennsylvania), Trenton (New Jersey), Dover (Delaware), Annapolis (Maryland), Washington, D.C., Charleston (West Virginia), Richmond (Virginia), Raleigh (North Carolina), Columbia (South Carolina), Atlanta (Georgia), Tallahassee (Florida)

Compass rose: North, South, East, West

Map Legend
- ✪ Country's capital
- ★ State capital
- — Border

Washington, D.C., is located north of Richmond, Virginia.

SOL 1.4c, 1.4d
*Additional information has been provided to enhance the Standards of Learning.

6 ■ Practice for Students

Name _____ Date _____

There are many places to visit in Washington, D.C.

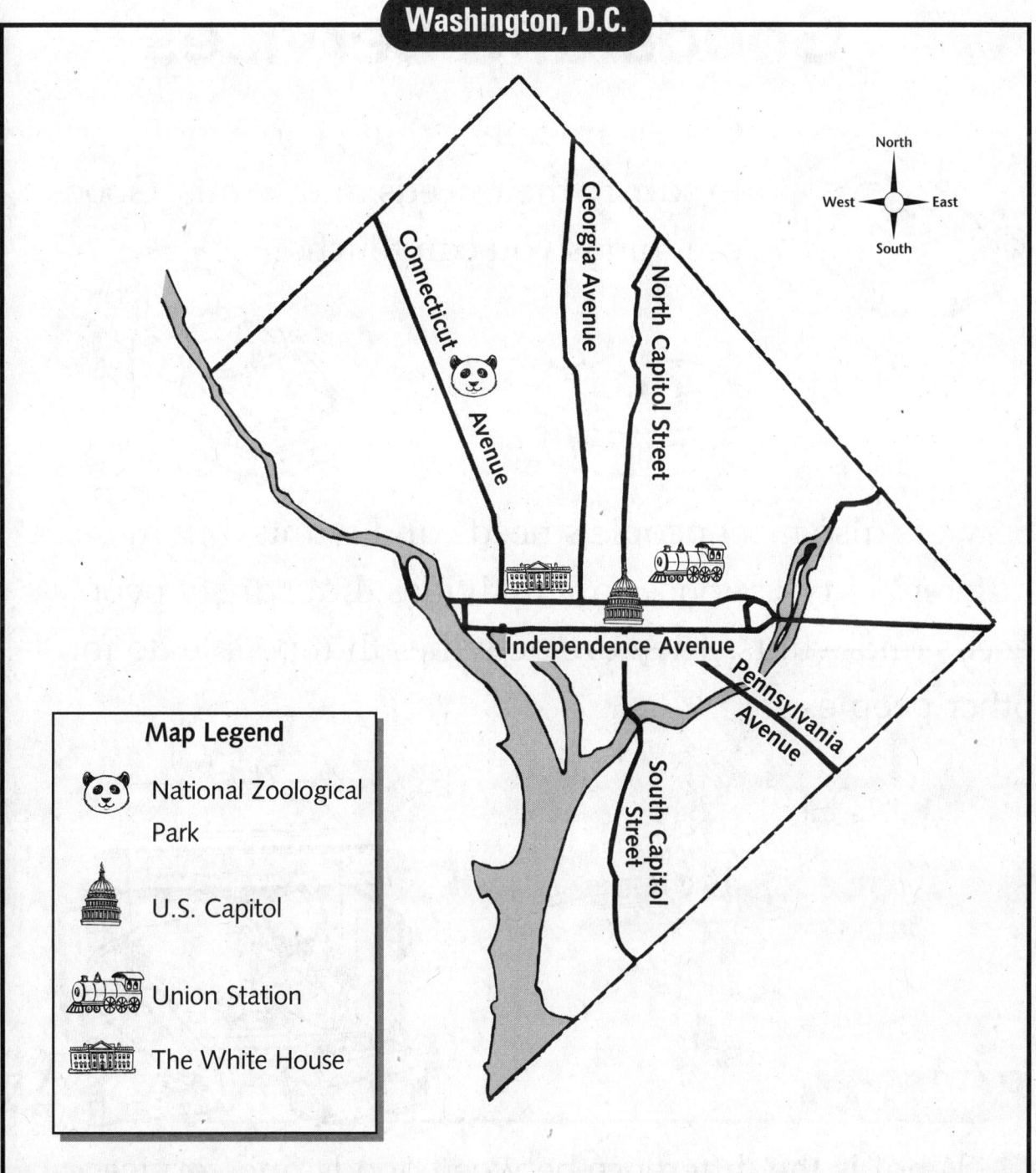

1. What is the symbol for Union Station?

2. What is north of the White House?

SOL 1.4c, 1.4d
*Additional information has been provided to enhance the Standards of Learning.

Practice for Students ■ 7

Name _____ Date _____

Difference Between Goods and Services

Goods are things that people make or use to satisfy their needs and wants. Goods are things you can touch.

Services also meet people's needs and wants, but in different ways. Services are activities that satisfy people's needs and wants. They are activities that people do for other people.

Review

1. What is the difference between goods and services?

2. Name three goods you used today.

   Draw a picture of a service you use.

8 ■ **Practice for Students**

SOL 1.7
*Additional information has been provided to enhance the Standards of Learning.

Name _____   Date _____

Spend or Save?

People can choose to spend or save money. Pam wants a new bicycle. She sees a ball at the store. If she buys the ball, she has to save more money for the bicycle.

Directions

Should Pam spend money for the ball, or should she save her money for the bicycle she wants? Why?

SOL 1.9
*Additional information has been provided to enhance the Standards of Learning.

Practice for Students ■ 9

Name _____ Date _____

People Are Buyers and Sellers

When you use money to buy a book or a ride on a bus, you are a buyer. Buyers use money to purchase goods or services.

When you sell your old comic books or wash the car to earn money, you are a seller. Sellers get money for selling goods or giving services.

Practice for Students

SOL 1.7
*Additional information has been provided to enhance the Standards of Learning.

Name _____ Date _____

In these pictures, who are the buyers? Who are the sellers?

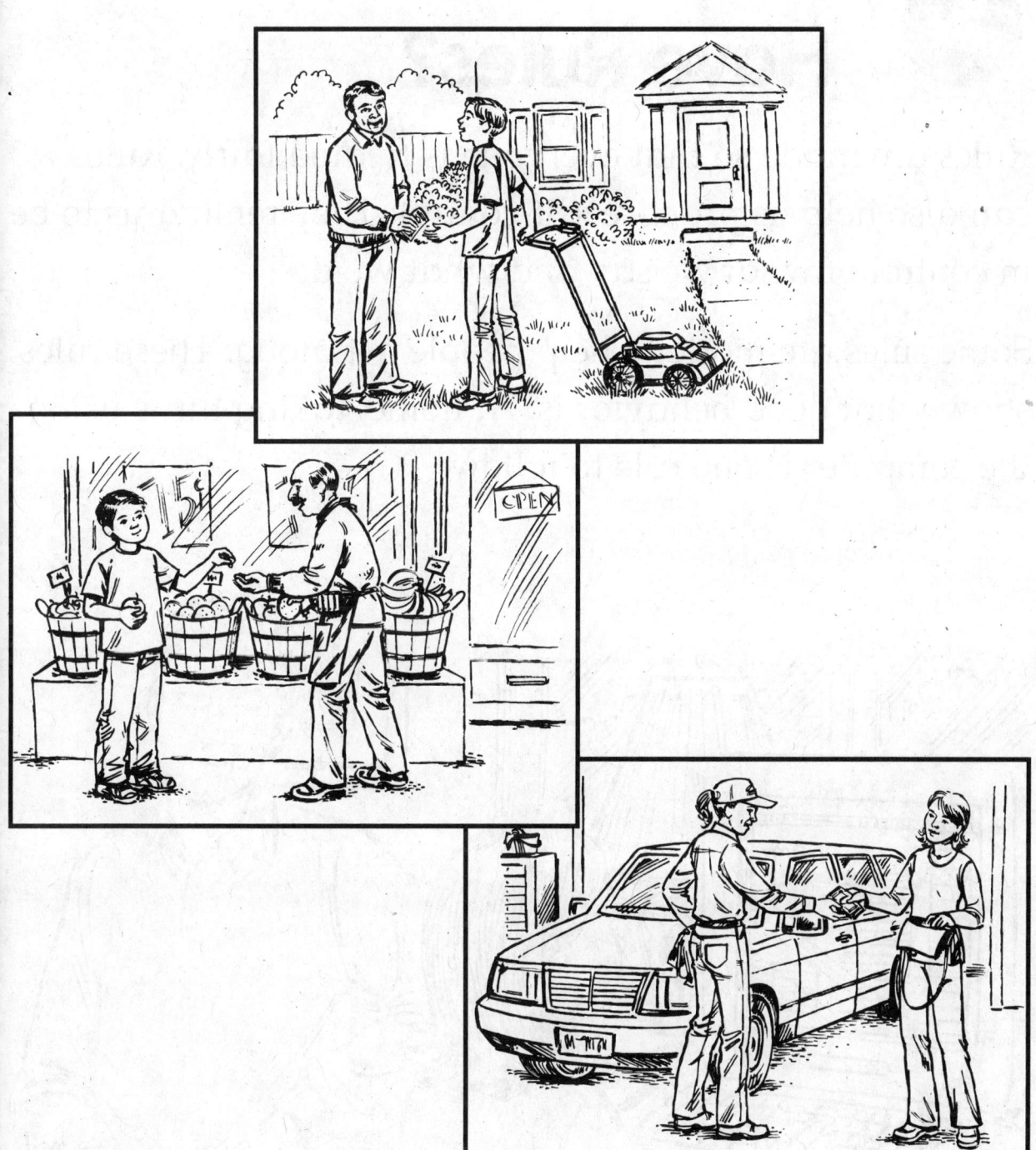

Directions

① Use blue to circle the buyers.

② Use red to circle the sellers.

Name _____ Date _____

Why Do We Have Rules?

Rules are made so that everyone is treated fairly. Rules can also help us practice self-control. They remind us to be in control of what we say and what we do.

Some rules are made to help people get along. These rules show what good behavior is. At home, taking turns using the computer is one rule to follow.

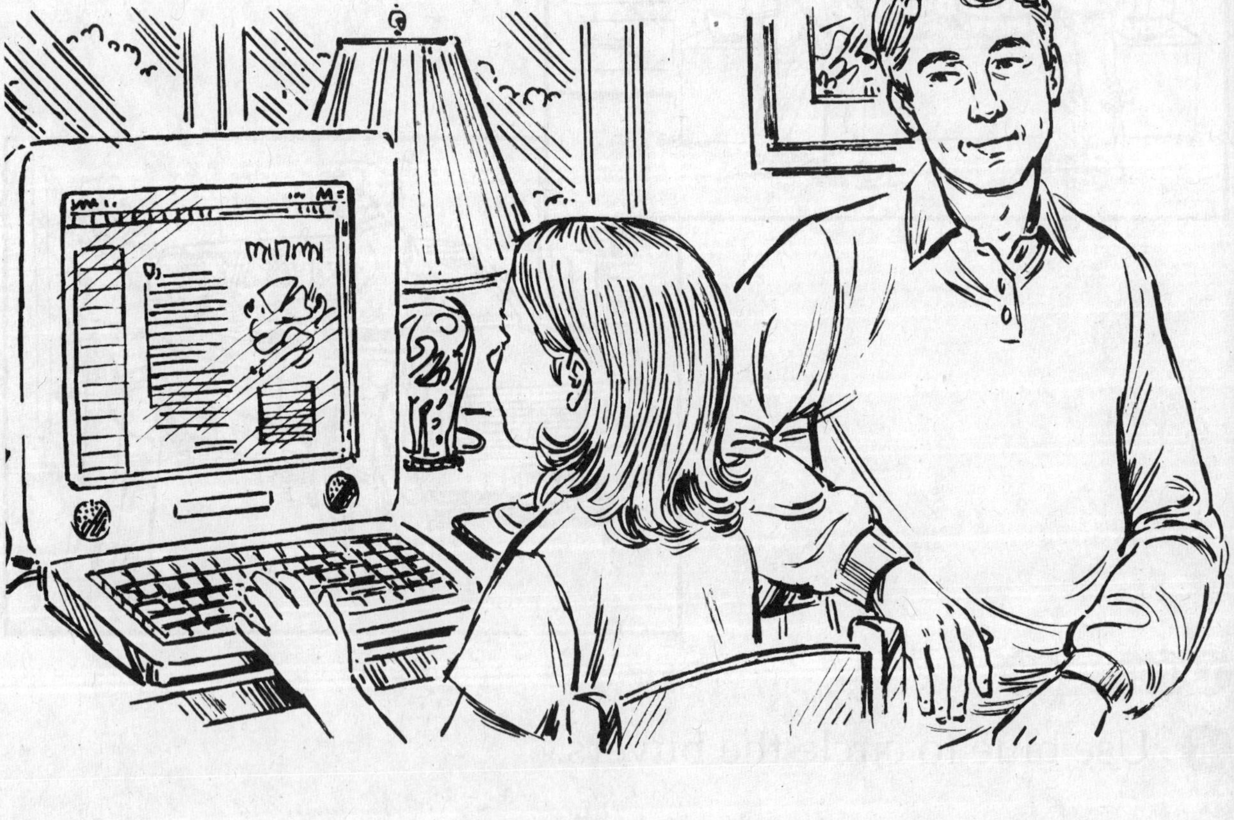

Name _____ Date _____

Some rules are made to keep people safe. At school, one rule tells you to walk, not run, in the hallways.

Other rules are made to protect the rights of all people. In some communities, one rule tells people to ride their bicycles on the sidewalk, not across someone's lawn.

Review

1. Why do we need rules?

2. How do you show self-control?

Draw a picture of a rule you have at home.

SOL 1.10b
*Additional information has been provided to enhance the Standards of Learning.

Practice for Students ■ 13

Name _____ Date _____

Being a Good Sport

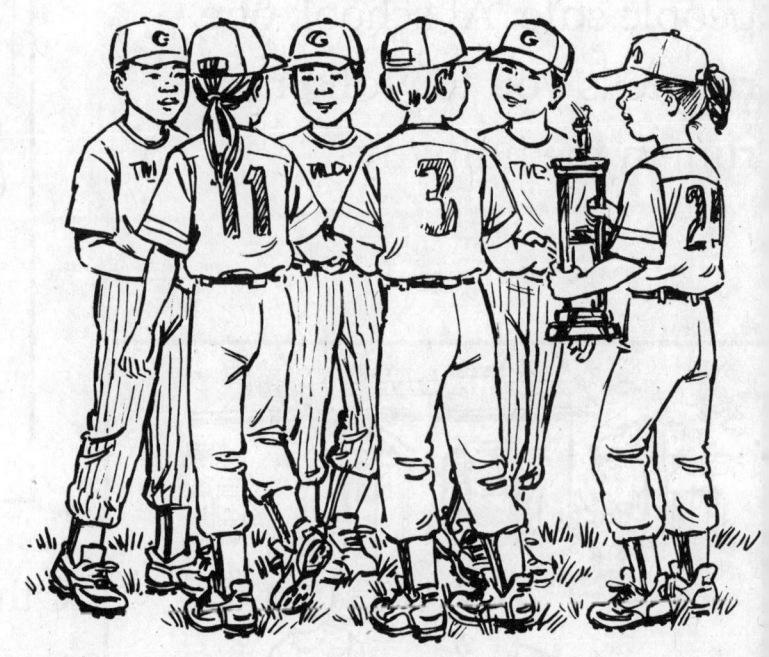

Being a good citizen is important, even when you play.

Good citizens play fairly. They follow the rules of the game. They wait their turns patiently. Good citizens also show good sportsmanship. They do not get angry or sad when they lose. They tell the winners, "Good game!"

Think of a game you like to play. How could you show good sportsmanship if you lose?

_____
_____
_____
_____

14 ■ Practice for Students

SOL 1.10a
*Additional information has been provided to enhance the Standards of Learning.

Name _____ Date _____

Showing Respect

Every person is important. Treating people with respect shows them they are important. When you respect others, they respect you.

Listening is one way to show respect.

Treating people and property with care is another way to show respect.

Review

1. Why should you show respect for people?

2. Why is listening a way to show respect?

Draw a picture of a way you can show respect for someone in your school.

SOL 1.10a
*Additional information has been provided to enhance the Standards of Learning.

Practice for Students ■ 15

Name _____ Date _____

Working Hard in School

We work hard in school.

We finish all of our work.

We listen to the teacher and other adult workers.

We keep our work places neat.

How do you work hard in school?

_____
_____
_____
_____

16 ■ Practice for Students

SOL 1.10c
*Additional information has been provided to enhance the Standards of Learning.

Name _____ Date _____

Taking Responsibility

We are responsible for what we do and for what we say at home, at school, and in the community.

Directions

1. Draw a red circle around the picture or pictures that show the boy being responsible for what he does.

2. Draw a blue circle around the picture or pictures that show the boy being responsible for what he says.

SOL 1.10d
*Additional information has been provided to enhance the Standards of Learning.

Practice for Students ■ 17

Name _____ Date _____

Honesty and Truthfulness

Good citizens should be honest and truthful. You should always tell the truth. People will believe you if you are honest. Listen to this story to see why it is important to show honesty and truthfulness.

The Boy Who Cried Wolf
a fable by Aesop

Once there was a boy who lived in a small village. His job was to watch the village sheep. Day after day he watched the sheep. One day he became bored. He thought of a way to have fun. The boy took a deep breath and yelled, "Wolf! Wolf! A wolf is chasing the sheep!"

The people from the village ran up the hill to help the boy. When they got to the top, they saw the boy and the sheep, but no wolf. The boy laughed and laughed when he saw the people angry and out of breath.

A man said, "You should not yell wolf if there is no wolf!" The villagers went back down the hill.

SOL 1.10e
*Additional information has been provided to enhance the Standards of Learning.

Name _____ Date _____

Soon the boy became bored again. He yelled "Wolf!" and laughed when the villagers ran up the hill again. A woman said, "You should not yell wolf when there is no wolf!" The villagers went back down the hill.

Later the boy saw a real wolf chasing the sheep. He stood up and yelled, "Wolf! Wolf! A wolf is chasing the sheep!" No one came. Soon the wolf had scared away all of the village sheep.

Review

1 Why did none of the villagers come the last time the boy yelled wolf?

2 Why is it important to show honesty and truthfulness?

What do you think the boy will do now? Write a story telling what happens next.

SOL 1.10e
*Additional information has been provided to enhance the Standards of Learning.

Practice for Students ■ 19

Name _____ Date _____

United as Americans

People celebrate American holidays in many ways. People in our community come from different origins and places around the world. They are united as Americans by common principles and traditions, such as celebrating Independence Day (Fourth of July) and pledging allegiance to the flag.

Seatack Elementary School, September 11, 2002

Directions

Draw a picture of your family celebrating an American holiday.

SOL 1.12
*Additional information has been provided to enhance the Standards of Learning.

20 ■ Practice for Students

Name _____ Date _____

Using a Time Line for Past and Present

Alexander Graham Bell made the first telephone in 1876. The telephone we use in the present looks very different from the telephone people used in the past.

This time line shows how the telephone has changed. The last picture on the right shows the telephone in the present. All of the pictures before that one show how telephones looked in the past.

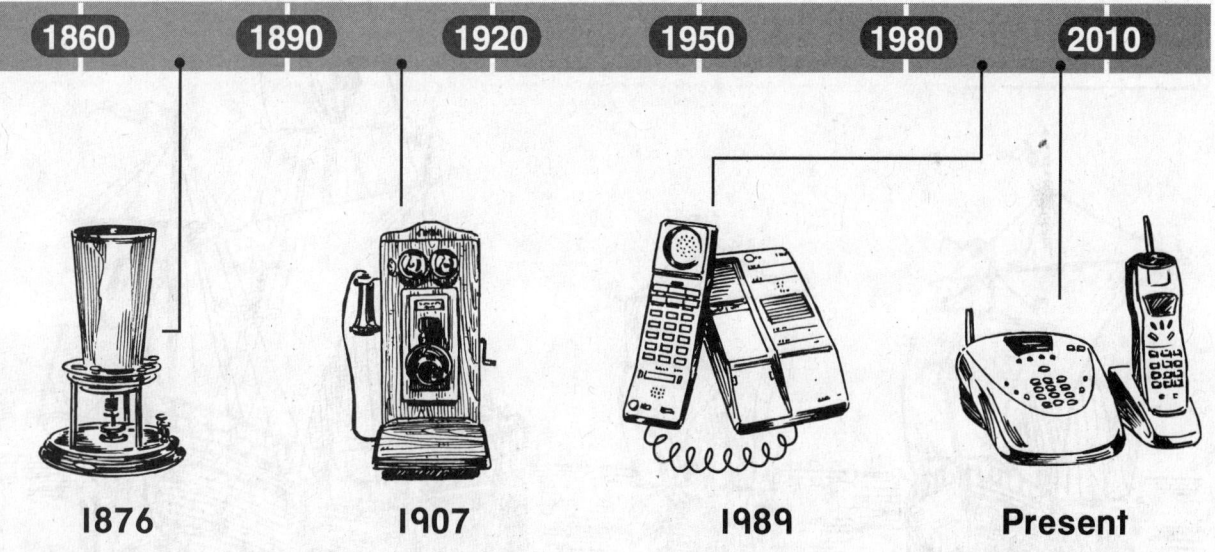

Directions

Find out about your past. Make a time line to show four events in your life. Draw pictures of the four events.

SOL 1.1
*Additional information has been provided to enhance the Standards of Learning.

Name _____ Date _____

Columbus Day

Christopher Columbus was an explorer. In 1492, he and his crew sailed away from Spain. They sailed on three ships called the Niña, the Pinta, and the Santa Maria. On October 12, after more than two months of sailing, they landed on an island in North America.

Name _____ Date _____

The people in Spain and other countries in Europe did not know about North America and South America. So Christopher Columbus is given credit for discovering America. We remember this important discovery in October with the holiday Columbus Day.

Some cities have big parades on Columbus Day.

Do you think Christopher Columbus and his crew were excited to see land after two months? Why?

_____
_____
_____
_____

SOL 1.3
*Additional information has been provided to enhance the Standards of Learning.

Practice for Students ■ 23

Name _____   Date _____

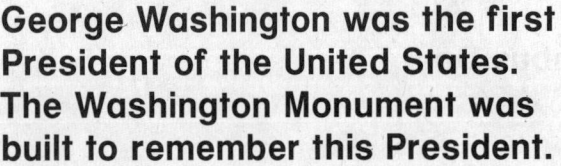

Presidents' Day

On Presidents' Day we remember all of the Presidents of the United States. We especially remember what President George Washington and President Abraham Lincoln did for our country. We celebrate this holiday in February.

George Washington was the first President of the United States. The Washington Monument was built to remember this President.

Abraham Lincoln was the sixteenth President of the United States. The Lincoln Memorial was built to remember this President.

Review

1. What are some ways we remember our Presidents?

2. Who is our President now?

 Write a letter to our President asking what things are part of the job of President.

SOL 1.3
*Additional information has been provided to enhance the Standards of Learning.

Name _____ Date _____

Independence Day (Fourth of July)

On July 4, 1776, America became a new country. We remember this special day every July 4 with the holiday Independence Day. This day is sometimes called America's birthday.

July

		1	2	3	④	5
6	7	8	9	10	11	12
13	14	15	16	17	18	19
20	21	22	23	24	25	26
27	28	29	30	31		

Review

1. When did America become a new country?

2. Why do you think we call Independence Day America's birthday?

Draw a picture of a way you like to celebrate Independence Day.

SOL 1.3
*Additional information has been provided to enhance the Standards of Learning.

Practice for Students ■ 25

Name _____ Date _____

Christopher Columbus

The explorer Christopher Columbus wanted to find a new route to get to Asia. In 1492, he sailed west from Spain to look for the new route.

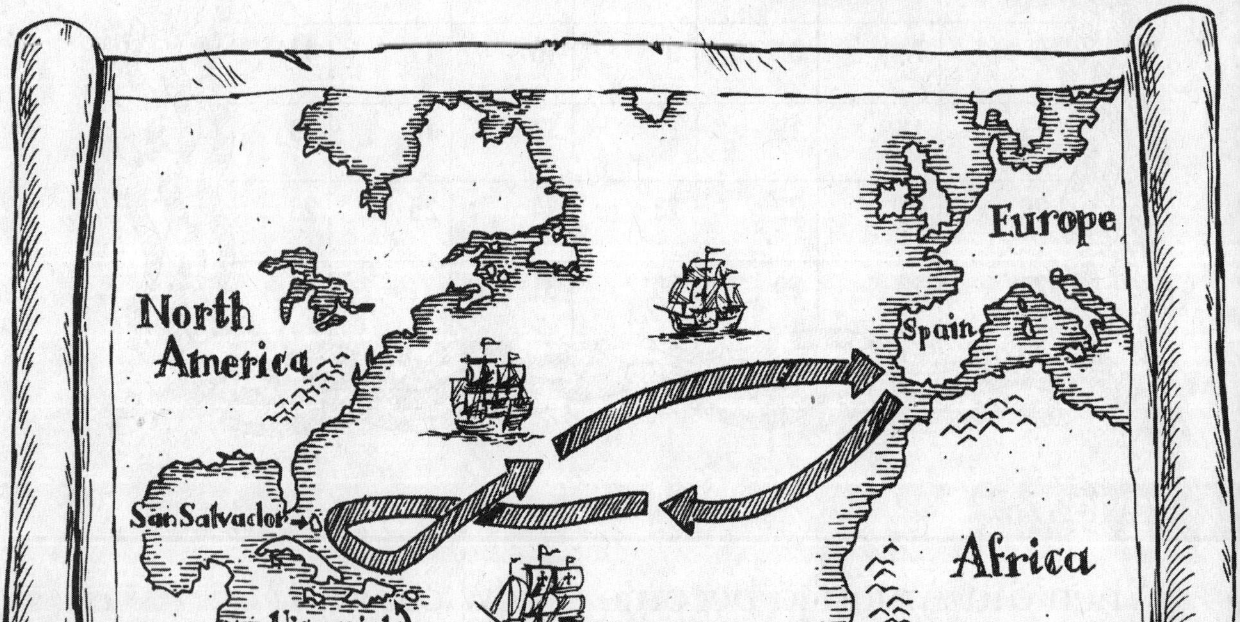

Columbus's route

SOL I.3
*Additional information has been provided to enhance the Standards of Learning.

26 ■ Practice for Students

Name _____ Date _____

Christopher Columbus and his crew did not reach Asia. They landed on an island in North America. They met the Taino people who lived there. The Tainos gave Columbus corn, peanuts, sweet potatoes, and tomatoes. He had never tasted these foods before.

Christopher Columbus returned to Spain. He talked about the people, the islands, and the foods he found. Soon many more people traveled to North America and South America.

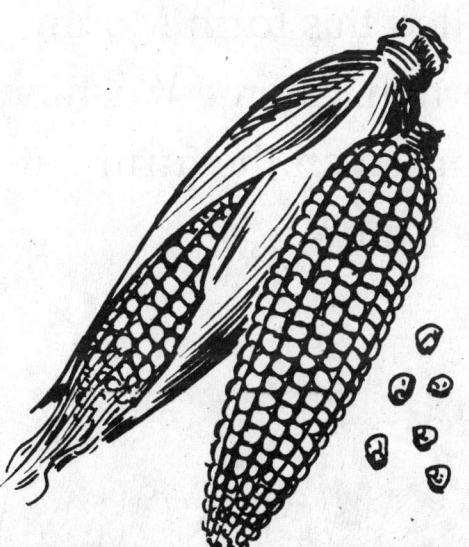

Directions

What do you think Christopher Columbus said to the people of Spain about his voyage? Tell a classmate what you would say if you were Christopher Columbus.

Name _____ Date _____

George Washington

George Washington was born in Virginia. When he was three years old, his family moved to a large farm in Virginia. They called this farm Mount Vernon. George Washington worked on the farm with his family.

Mount Vernon

SOL 1.2
*Additional information has been provided to enhance the Standards of Learning.

28 ■ **Practice for Students**

Name _____ Date _____

George Washington later became a brave leader. He led soldiers when Americans fought a war to be free from England.

A few years after the war, Americans chose a President. George Washington became the first President of the United States. He is known as the "Father of Our Country." After he was President, he went back to being a farmer at Mount Vernon.

1 Why do you think people chose George Washington as the first President?

_____
_____
_____
_____

2 What was George Washington known as?

_____
_____
_____
_____

SOL 1.2
*Additional information has been provided to enhance the Standards of Learning.

Benjamin Franklin

Benjamin Franklin was a great leader in the early days of our country. He wanted to make people's lives better. He started the first volunteer fire department in Philadelphia, Pennsylvania. The library he started there was also the first in the country.

The Library Company in Philadelphia

Name _____ Date _____

Benjamin Franklin was also a scientist. In June 1752, he did an experiment. He tied a metal key to the end of a kite string. Then he flew the kite during a thunderstorm. His experiment showed that lightning is a form of electricity.

Review

1. What did Benjamin Franklin start in Philadelphia, Pennsylvania?

2. What was Benjamin Franklin trying to prove with his kite experiment?

   Where is your school library? What does it look like? Draw a picture of your school library.

Name _____ Date _____

Abraham Lincoln

Abraham Lincoln was born in a log cabin in Kentucky. When he was a young boy, his family moved to Indiana.

Abraham Lincoln went to school for only one year. He taught himself how to read, write, and do math. Later he read law books and became a lawyer. He was known as "Honest Abe."

Abraham Lincoln reading to his son

Name _____ Date _____

Abraham Lincoln became the sixteenth President of the United States. We remember him with statues, stamps, and even money.

Abraham Lincoln's picture is on some of our money.

1 Do you think it was easy for Abraham Lincoln to learn to read without going to school? Why?

_____
_____
_____
_____

2 What was Abraham Lincoln known as?

_____
_____
_____
_____

SOL 1.2
*Additional information has been provided to enhance the Standards of Learning.

Practice for Students ■ 33

George Washington Carver

When George Washington Carver was young, he was often sick. He could not help with the heavy work his family had to do on the farm. So he collected plants and studied them and learned how to care for them.

When he was older, George Washington Carver became a teacher. He kept studying plants and science. He used what he learned to find a way to help farmers who had poor soil on their farms. George Washington Carver showed farmers that growing peanuts, sweet potatoes, and soybeans made the soil rich again.

Name _____ Date _____

Soon there were more peanuts, sweet potatoes, and soybeans than people could eat. George Washington Carver discovered hundreds of ways to use these foods besides eating them.

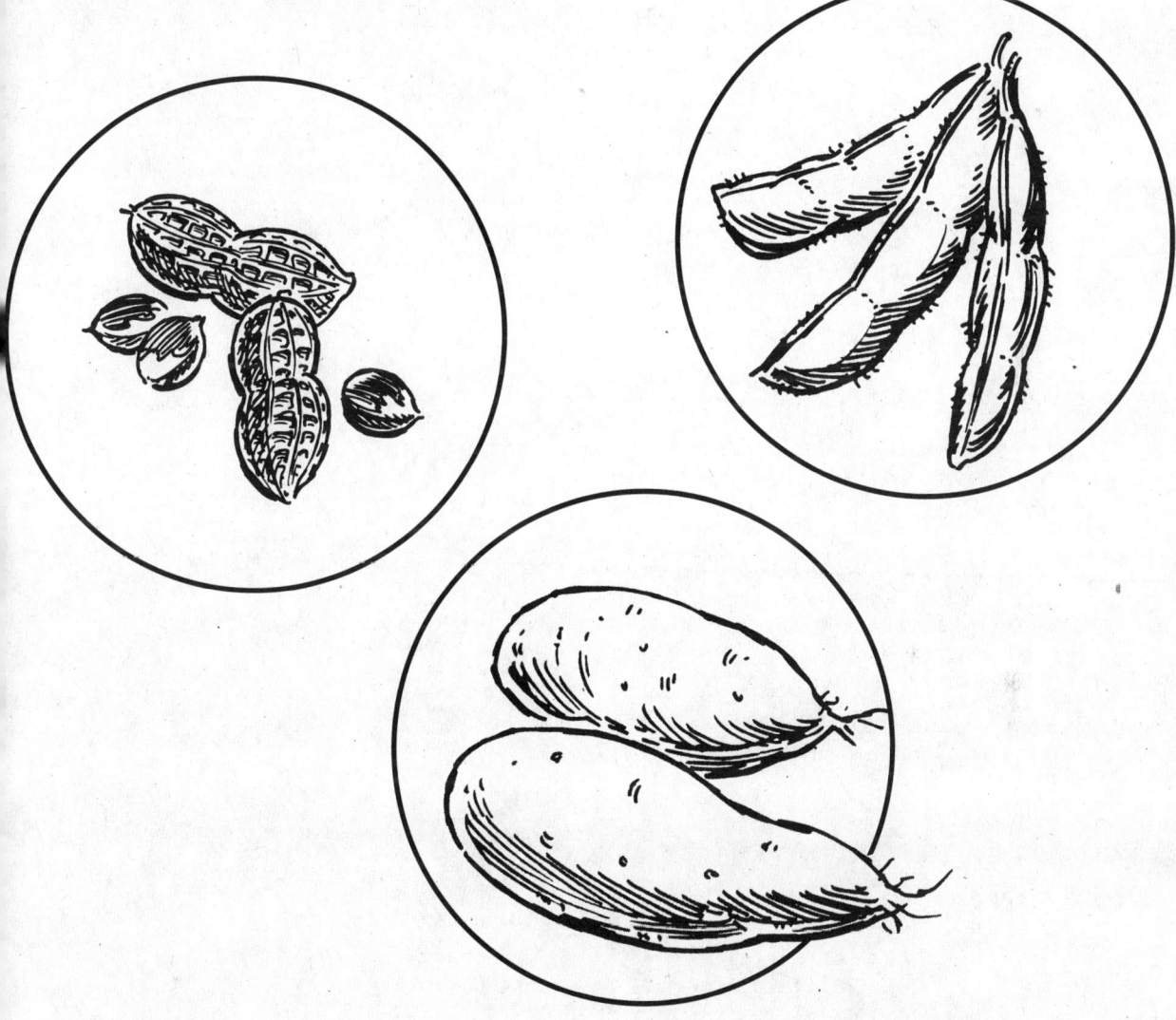

Some of the things that George Washington Carver made from peanuts are ink, dyes, soap, and shampoo.

Directions

Find out how peanuts grow. Make a poster showing what you find.

SOL 1.2
*Additional information has been provided to enhance the Standards of Learning.